THE INDIE AUTHOR BESTIARY II

AN EPIC QUEST AGAINST THE BEASTS OF THE WRITING WORLD

M.L. RONN

CONTENTS

RETURN TO MYTHIA

WHAT YOU'LL LEARN FROM THIS BOOK

When I wrote the *Indie Author Bestiary*, I thought it would be a one-and-done book.

After all, how many more "beasts" of the writing world could there be?

I was wrong.

It turns out there are far more beasts than I could have ever imagined when I wrote the first book.

In many respects, the first *Indie Author Bestiary* was about winning the war with yourself. There are so many emotions we wrestle with when we become writers; many of those emotions stick with us on our writing journeys.

But there are more beasts we must face once we have won the war with ourselves.

What about the war against others? Writing is a solitary profession, but everyone has an opinion about it. Often, we find ourselves in a battle of expectations—often those of others.

The second volume of the *Indie Author Bestiary* deals with those beasts we face once we become comfortable in our own skins and let the world know it.

So take up your sword again, fellow writer. More beasts await you.

—M.L. Ronn
Des Moines, Iowa
September 29, 2022

THE SHORES OF ISOLATION

You awaken on a beach to the sound of rocky waves. Seagulls wheel under a dark gray sky, squawking as they disappear into the heavy, ominous clouds.

The sand shifts beneath you as you sit up. It is as fine as velvet and prickly as iron filings.

Pain explodes on the left side of your head. Your armor clanks as you raise a hand and feel wet blood.

Blood. Your hand is stained with blood...

Your shield lies next to you. Its insignia of a book is scratched and faded from your many battles. In the shield's metallic reflection, you see a large gash on your forehead.

You sit on the beach, staring at the choppy waves that make the ocean look as if it is foaming at the mouth. There is only an endless horizon of gray, the squawking of seagulls, and the fog of war.

You walk down the beach with your sword and shield slung on your back. Every bone in your body aches as you try to remember.

Slowly, images stream across your mind's eye.

The giant stone Tower of Laughing Beasts that stretches into the clouds. Your mentor, Michael, clad in armor and marching next to you as you stormed the premises. The devilish, macabre faces of the beasts you slaughtered. A faded, worn leather-skin journal that Michael gave you, each page a meditation with sage advice. Michael sitting in an archway, wounded by the beast Self-Doubt, staring at the beautiful sky as he took his last breath…

The wound on your head won't let itself be ignored. A lightning bolt of pain surges through your skull as you remember the face of Self-Doubt, the beast at the top of the tower.

You drew your sword, you vowed to avenge Michael, and you ran at the beast with every force of your being, crusading against it in the name of writers everywhere.

The beast's face is a great blur. You cannot remember your battle with it, only that it cast you from the top of the tower and into the sea. That's how you ended up here.

You pause and take in your surroundings. Along the shore, you spot a glint of metal. A human skeleton is clad in armor. You look away. The endless ocean brings you only despair, so you turn inward to a forest shrouded in shadows and mist.

The only thing that matters now is your survival. You start toward the forest when a familiar voice calls your name.

A phantasm blinds you with resplendent golden light. As your eyes adjust, you gaze upon the brown face of an old friend. Michael smiles and says, "It is good to see you again, fellow writer."

You listen closely as Michael tells you his tale.

⊏⊐

We are reunited again, fellow writer!

I didn't think we would see each other until it was your time to transition into the great beyond, but it appears the universe had plans for another reunion.

I died a happy man. I am grateful for the time we spent together while I was in the flesh. When Self-Doubt mortally wounded me atop the Tower of Laughing Beasts, I died with no regrets.

You and I both had a taste of death in our battle with the beast Desperation, so I was ready. The afterlife is exactly what you think it will be—honeyed light, communion with every writer that has ever lived, and the best food you've ever had!

I was having coffee with Ray Bradbury when, all of a sudden, my body glowed with a strange golden light. Ray raised his coffee and said, "Live forever!" and the next thing I knew, I was here on this beach.

This ghost form isn't so bad. Look how I float. Now that I think about it, feet always were an inconvenience I never considered. It appears we must journey forth again.

Where we are—your guess is as good as mine, fellow writer. The Tower of Laughing Beasts lies yonder. Trust me that we do not want to return there.

I am not familiar with the land we walk in now. Keep your wits about you. Your injuries look bad, but they are not grave. Self-Doubt wounded you, but it did not kill you, so you live to fight again.

As a reminder, let's go over tools in your arsenal:

- a **sword** imbued with the magical residue of words,
- **actions** that move your writing life forward,
- a **shield** of knowledge,
- **armor** forged with positive thinking and optimism,
- a **dragon** who will give you resourcefulness and a second wind in the face of true adversity.

Now that we have reviewed your arsenal, we should explore this strange place so that we may find the way home.

Fellow writer, look out!

That was close. Did you see that giant purple tentacle that reached out from the sea to grab you?

That was a familiar beast—the beast Fear. It has tracked you across the sea and wants a rematch.

Look alive, fellow writer! The tentacle comes out of the water again.

BEAST #22: FEAR (REDUX)

This beast is unkillable. Remember, we encountered it many times during our journey up the Tower of Laughing Beasts. It won't give up, so we should show it that we won't give up either.

Steady your sword and slash at the first opportunity.

Slash! Slash!

That's it, fellow writer! You have cut the tentacle into cubes and it slithers dying on the sand.

To your left—another tentacle sprouts from the sea.

I will summon our dragons. Fortunately for you, my trusty dragon is now at your command. Though you were unsuccessful in destroying the Tower of Laughing Beasts, you gained another ally in resourcefulness. I'd say that's quite metaphorical, don't you?

The dragons circle the sands. Dragons, let forth your flames!

There—success. Our beast's tentacles are burning like cooked meat. I do not feel sorry for it.

And right on time—the third tentacle wishes to tango. Shield up!

SHING!

That impact was hard, but you must get up before the tentacle comes back around to finish you off.

To your feet like a true knight. Here it comes again. Shield up and parry with a hearty slash.

Slash!

Our beast's tentacle writhes in death.

You are brave to pick it up and verify that it is dead. The suckers attach to your armor. They pull off with stubborn plops.

I can finally relax. Here on this beach, in the constant roar of the sea and sea spray on our faces, we can finally rest from fear, but I suggest we keep moving, for this beast has unlimited tentacles.

Do you still have the journal I gave you?

Excellent. I trust that you have internalized the lessons I passed down to you, but I have a feeling there are more lessons to learn—lessons that you must write, fellow writer. Take your quill and let us philosophize together on the first available blank page...

A Meditation for Fear (Redux)

Fear is an ever-morphing and omnipresent foe. You can never get rid of it; you can only stave it off for a time. It will always return no matter what you do, and it will always show up unannounced at the worst time.

Though it is an ever-morphing foe, its weaknesses are the same:

- **Action**. Fear strives to stop you from taking action. The moment you take action, it has no hold over you.
- **Words**. As long as you keep writing, fear will retreat. Fear despises progress in your work, and with every word you write, it swears to return with revenge twofold.
- **Resourcefulness**. Fear doesn't like when you think out of the box. Sometimes, this breeds more fear, but by daring to be courageous, you will weaken it.

With the help of our friends and comrades, fear cannot realize its dreams; in its retreat, we realize ours.

BEAST #23: UNCERTAINTY

Congratulations on writing your first meditation, fellow writer. It is quite a compliment and a signal that you are improving your skill and understanding as an author. Any time we face a beast from now on, we will stop and perform that exercise. It is for your own good in the long run. Before long, your journal will rival mine.

Do you hear that song, fellow writer?

Something is upon us. Something is singing—a woman's voice, soft and soothing.

Why, I've never heard such a beautiful thing in my life. I am enthralled...

You're walking toward the sea. Let me float with you. We must discover the source of this gentle song.

We must be getting closer because I hear words in the song. It is singing, "Come here, come here, swim with me..."

I don't know who the figure is, but swimming sounds very good right now. If only I had my physical form—I would wade into the water with you and we would enjoy these cold, choppy waters with sharks and jellyfish.

Wait. What did I just say? I must be losing my mind...

Such a beautiful song… She asks us to submerge and meet her on the ocean floor where we will reside… Forever??

Fellow writer, this is a trap! Do not put your head in that water. I would take your hand, but I'm a ghost, remember?

Don't make me slap you. Blasted hounds, I couldn't slap you even if I wanted. Very well, I will yell until you listen to me. Stop walking. Ignore her. This is a beast!

There, I convinced you. Run back into the sand, into safety. Let us gaze upon the face of this new beast who confronts us.

Quite curious. I can see no beast. Can you? All I see is the abounding ocean and packs of clouds moving in from above. Our beast does not want to be seen.

Perhaps our beast doesn't truly exist.

The song is fading. Now she is screaming at us. She is calling us curse words, telling us that we are fools.

I shudder to think how many writers are dead at the bottom of the ocean with her. Let's get out of here, fellow writer. The further away we go, the safer we'll be.

Write your meditation when we get into the woods.

A Meditation for Uncertainty

Beware the siren song of uncertainty. It is a beast that controls you from beyond.

No matter how many beasts you have conquered, you will one day end up on the shores of isolation. You will battle with fear and succeed. Then, one day, you will need to make a decision and you won't know where to start. The information you need will be unavailable, and you will feel as if you are on a razor blade, with success on one end and failure on the other. The only difference between the two is luck.

Uncertainty will sing to you and intoxicate you. You won't

know what to do other than to sway like a cobra to the rhythm of Uncertainty's song. Sway too long and you will find yourself at the bottom of the sea.

We are all taken by Uncertainty's song from time to time. The key is to recognize when we are swaying. The sooner we recognize it, the sooner we can break her spell.

Sometimes, the best thing to do in light of limited information is to trust our gut, act with conviction, and be kind to ourselves if our decision doesn't get us the result we planned for.

Perhaps writing that book wasn't as successful as you thought it would be. Or, the marketing campaign you thought would catapult your book up the charts fails miserably. Or, you choose a cover that doesn't sell.

The reality is that in an alternate universe, you could be wildly successful if you had made just one decision differently. That's painful to think about. Visualizing ourselves in these different dimensions is what causes uncertainty. No one wants to end up in the dimension where they fail, but failure is an excellent teacher.

Be decisive in all things you do, own your decisions, and learn from them.

THE FOREST OF ILLUSION

Let us flee into this darkened forest.

This place is something out of a nightmare. If it weren't for the light of my soul, you would barely be able to see your hand in front of your face. The air is stuffy and intoxicatingly dank. Many of these trees may have never seen humans. Their gnarled chocolate bark isn't the kind I would put in my fireplace, I can tell you that.

Though we are many yards from the shore now, these trees block out all sound. You would never know we were so close to the beach.

Keep your hand near your sword. I don't like this place.

It would be beautiful if it weren't so ominous. The way the light slants down from the trees, the tittering of strange parrots, and the occasional whiff of verdant flowers—simply stunning. But sometimes beauty is deadly.

I have been to a place like this. They were the woods of another land. The locals called them Fearwoods. Your shadow roamed among them. I don't mean your actual shadow, but the shadow of your Self. The real you that would scare you if you truly met it. The shadow would ambush you when you least expected it.

The only way to survive the Fearwoods was to hurry through them. Though these woods are different, we would do well not to tarry.

You may not believe this, fellow writer, but I also wrote a book with evil woods in it. Imagine a teddy bear knight with a sword and shield venturing through a whispering forest with malicious trees that rearrange themselves to fool him and keep him in the forest forever. I suppose that is why I also get a bad feeling about woods like this.

⊏⊐

It has been at least one hour since we entered these woods. So many of these trees look the same. We could turn back if we wanted, but that way lies madness. Fear would almost surely try to kill us again, or you might fall prey to Uncertainty's song. It is better to keep going.

A-ha! We have come upon a foot path. Perhaps it portends a positive sign.

Let us walk as the hours pass, telling stories about our writing and our books.

This is one terribly long path. I wonder how long it goes.

Well, what an interesting turn of fortune. A man is sitting against a tree just off the path over there. I almost missed him because his green tunic blends in with the foliage. He is eating a meal of bread and beans. Let's engage him and see what he knows.

The man has a face lined with sorrow. His gray hair has seen more colorful days.

"A traveler? What a rare surprise!"

The man grins and bids us to sit with him.

"I was just about to start a fire. If you would bring me some tender, I will be glad to share a meal with you and tell you what I know."

It is a good thing this man cannot see me. To see a ghost in such a spooky forest would send him running. I will let you do the talking, but I will chime in when needed. Go and fetch him some tinder and let us enjoy a moment of respite.

"Thank you for the tinder, my dear knight. It has been a long time since I have seen a knight not bearing the insignia of the crown. Crown, you ask…You must truly be a foreigner. Everyone knows the royal family of Mythia, the land in which you walk. The king is well-known and respected throughout the land. This civilization has flourished for hundreds of years. That is, until tragedy befell the royal family. God bless the king, and heaven help the royals abducted by those blasted beasts."

Beasts… Though this may be a strange land, fellow writer, we know something about beasts, don't we?

"Yes, beasts roam these lands. You must be careful not to travel at night, for that is when they come out. But they will attack you during the day if you're their preferred prey. You came from the Tower of Laughing Beasts, you say? I have heard of that place, yes. A dreadful place to spend one's time, I'd say. What business do you have in such a place?"

I would tell him, but I suppose you must do the talking.

Our fellow traveler strokes his chin. He is intrigued by your superb storytelling ability.

"You are just the kind of person who can survive in Mythia. With your battle skills and your mental fortitude, you will get along here just fine. Me, you ask? I am a weary traveler. The king has hired me to survey the land. I must venture to every corner of this land once a fortnight and return with a report of any developments. As you will find out, while this is a beautiful land with beautiful people, it has had its turmoil. The beasts have overrun certain areas and even turned some of the king's former loyal subjects against him. They will surely be against you too. The fire is crackling quite nicely now. I have brought with me a leg of lamb and I would be happy to share it with you. I have enough provisions for more than a fortnight because I enjoy coming across new people. As they say in my village, the best way to prevent an enemy is to put food in his stomach."

———

"That meal was good! I hope you enjoyed it. The seasoning on that lamb is from a pouch I've received from His Majesty himself. When you meet him, I am sure he will be glad to serve you a meal that you can eat to your heart's content. I must go to sleep now. I would love to chat with you, but I must rise at dawn and continue my journey. Please allow me to give you some advice. These woods are not what they seem. You have a few more hours' walk before the beasts will appear. Whatever you do, I strongly recommend that you do not engage them with your weapons. That will make them angry and they will respond in kind. Do not strike first. That is the mark of a fool and a foreigner. Always let the beast make the first move, and you may respond accordingly. You will gain the advantage when they show their skills. You have fought many beasts, so you can handle a fight, but the beasts here are of a different flavor. Keep your wits about you and you just might survive. Farewell, gentle traveler."

BEAST #24: BAD ADVICE

What a fine companion to spend a few hours with.

I am suspicious—I still don't like these woods—but that traveler has done us a great service today. If this King of Mythia is as good of a man as the traveler says, then he is a credit to this kingdom. We must never forget his kindness.

The sun is falling. The crickets sing and the light through the canopy has brightened into that bone-white glow that we know so well. According to our fellow traveler, it is now prime beast time.

I am intrigued by the Kingdom of Mythia. It is good to know that there are friendly faces in this land. Once we glimpse the faces of the evil ones, we will have a true picture of Mythia.

Fellow writer, quiet. Did you hear that? Someone is snoring —no, *something* is snoring. Look how your armor rattles every few seconds. Whatever it is, it is big, and it is close.

There is its tail, a gray, leathery mass among exposed tree roots. If we follow this tale through the shrubbery, we see a four-legged monstrosity with two heads, antlers, snaggle-fangs that protrude over wine-red lips, and claws sharp enough to cut through your armor. This is a formidable beast indeed. I estimate that it is three men long and two men tall.

Our fellow traveler told us to keep moving and ignore these beasts. If they strike, we will let them strike first. But you shouldn't use your weapons.

It appears discretion is the better part of valor tonight. Let's creep away…

Oh no. You stepped on a bundle of twigs, fellow writer. The beast is waking up. It has opened its jaundiced eyes and is looking around the forest for the source of the sound.

Blasted hounds! It sees us. Its roar is ferocious and bone-shaking. It is standing on all four feet now. I was wrong about my estimations. This beast is four men tall! Sword at the ready!

You must concentrate as he staggers toward you.

Remember what our fellow traveler said. We must let the beast strike first.

Stay calm. We will persevere through this battle just as we persevered through the Tower of Laughing Beasts. We are a dynamic duo.

Oh my. It appears that this beast is not just one beast. It is connected to several others. Their eyes glow through the thicket. Their tails are connected. We have made a grave miscalculation.

The beast is lunging! Good dodge, fellow writer.

Slash!

The beasts are circling us now. This is not good. There is too much tree cover for us to call our dragons. This is going to be a straight-out brawl. I wish I were there to fight with you. The best I can do is guide you, fellow writer.

The beast on your left—strike its flank!

Spin around and stab the one behind you in the eye.

That vine over there—use it to swing onto the third beast's back. Stab the fleshy white spot on its neck.

The beast is screaming now. You've wounded it. We'll see if the wound is mortal.

Jump down and seek cover under that fallen tree. The beasts are distracted.

They're circling the screaming beast. Rivers of magenta blood run down its body. It is screaming so loudly that I can see its flesh-colored gums. That blow was a good one, fellow writer.

The beasts kneel to the wounded one. Are they paying their respects? No—they are going to sleep. No! They too are dying!

The screaming beast is no longer screaming. It lies on the forest floor, the last glimmers of life draining from its opal-colored eyes. The remaining beasts are dead too, as if they died of a broken heart.

What a turn of events. It appears this battle is over.

I hope that impact didn't permanently mess you up, fellow writer. The beast hit you hard. While you were lying there, I was concerned that it might have been the end for you. Your armor would have failed under that beast's hoof. But we are lucky that you live.

Our hail fellow well met gave us bad advice. He told us to wait until the beasts strike and not to use our weapons. We let the beasts strike first, but if we hadn't used our weapons, the beast would be the one claiming victory right now.

If we had struck the first beast while it slept, we would have killed all the beasts simultaneously.

I don't know what types of beasts our traveler has been fighting, but either he was outright lying to us or he was an incompetent warrior.

Which is it?

You believe it was incompetence, then. I shall take the opposite tack. No one would give such bad advice to a warrior. He knew we were warriors, and yet he told us to be passive in the face of this beast. I didn't realize how bad his advice was at the time, but if I had, I would have had you say something.

Do you truly believe it was just incompetence, fellow writer? I'm not so sure. Unfortunately, we'll never know. But if we encounter that traveler again, we're going to have some choice words for him, aren't we?

Let's write our meditation.

A Meditation for Bad Advice

Everyone has advice. Everyone loves to give advice freely. Sometimes, the advice is well taken; other times, it is not.

There are three types of advice:

1. **Advice that's meant for you**. This advice is right on time and perfect for your situation when you hear it.
2. **Advice that is not meant for you**. This advice is a bad fit for your situation *at any time*.
3. **Advice that you're not ready for yet**. This advice may seem like a bad fit, but it will be a good fit in time.

True wisdom is knowing what type of advice you are receiving at any time.

Most advice is bad advice. Advice that we're not ready for yet is more frequent than we think. But good advice—the advice that helps you take your skills to the next level—is the rarest of all. You must search for it like a lost diamond ring in a big forest. You walk and walk and walk, and just when you think you aren't going to find it, a glimmer on the forest floor catches your eye.

Develop a filter for advice. Ask yourself if advice is appropriate for you and your situation at the time. Also, ask how the advice feels. If something doesn't feel good, it's probably not a fit. Some mentors challenge us to do things we didn't think we could do, but there's a difference between that and advice that tries to shoehorn you into a particular activity, such as a marketing style that doesn't jibe with your aesthetic.

Good advice is advice that makes you think "Wow, I never considered that," or "Wow, why didn't I think of that to begin with?" Good advice helps you realize your true potential.

Because everyone has advice and loves to give it freely, we are oversaturated with it. Some advice-givers are indeed bad actors, but most often, they're just trying to help people in their own way, and they don't understand the impact that their advice would have on you personally. Therefore, it is your responsibility to develop a filter.

Filter out bad advice and you will gain clarity and calm.

BEAST #25: OBSTINACY

Our journey through this evil forest continues.

I know you're still sulking about our encounter with that traveler, but there is nothing we can do about it.

I struck a nerve. Do you truly disagree with me about the status of that traveler?

As I said, I believe he was a bad actor. You do not. It is okay to have disagreements—oh come on, fellow writer, why won't you talk to me? He did strike me as a decent fellow, but there are a lot of bad guys who are decent fellows in the right circumstances.

If you still won't talk to me, I'll give you some space and we can forget about the encounter. At least we are alive to disagree.

These trees irritate me. You would think that as you travel through the forest, their makeup would change or give us clues that we might be reaching the end. But every hour, it feels like we have been moving in circles.

Wait—something is afoot.

I hear laughing. Soft, malicious laughter, as subtle as the rustling of leaves.

It's gone now. Keep your hand near your sword.

———

I wonder how late it is. We shouldn't stop until sunrise. This way, we won't be ambushed by beasts.

These damned trees still look the same. I could have sworn we passed that same tree with an arrow notch on it an hour ago. There it is again.

I hate this place.

———

An hour is a long time to walk in silence. If you are still angry with me, then get over it, fellow writer. Until I am called back to the afterlife, we are stuck together.

At least we're making progress in the forest. Things seem to be a little different now. The vines don't hang quite the same way and the clearings seem a little bigger. Thank goodness for that. We might just find our way out of this forest by sunrise.

Or not. There's that same tree again with the arrow mark...

And there is that laughter again.

Someone is among us. Call out into the darkness—who's there?

We'll wait for our foe to reveal itself. Draw your sword.

Fire!

That tree over there has exploded in magical fire. Triangular eyes and a nightmarish mouth speak to us through the fire.

"Travelers, you will never leave this forest."

We'll see about that, evil tree.

"No matter how long or far you walk, we will be with you."

The surrounding trees are erupting in fire too. They glow

so brightly that it looks as if we are in the middle of a wildfire. The heat is as intense as a forge.

"We love to hear you bicker. That is how most travelers end up in this place. Thank goodness there are two of you. If you were solo, we would rend you to shreds."

Solo… This beast is a collective organism too. It thrives on relationships.

"Keep walking, travelers. Let us hear you fight even harder. We will provide the drab scenery for your trifle."

They *want* us to fight. This whole thing has been a trap. I told you I hated this place.

What's that, fellow writer? You apologize?

I apologize too. We shouldn't have gotten into a fight over something so silly.

"No! You foolish knights! Keep fighting!"

The fire in the trees smolders. The fire is dying. The beast *is* the fire. We will watch as it crackles to death and dies on the forest floor.

That was a close one. Let's write our meditation.

A Meditation for Obstinacy

When we make up our minds to do something, sometimes we set out to do it no matter the consequences. We don't realize that we are charging down the wrong path. Others see our escapade for what it is and try to warn us, but we don't listen. Only during a low moment do we gain clarity about what we've done. At that point, there are two possible reactions: shame or anger.

Those who feel shame wear it like a battle scar. Sometimes, the shame is so great that writers quit.

Anger causes us to lash out at those trying to warn us.

Where things get complicated is whether you are traveling down the right path and whether the people warning you are giving good advice.

There is a thin line between obstinacy and dogged determination.

A writer who is doggedly determined eventually succeeds. Their failure to listen to others and insistence on doing things their way is what ultimately makes them successful. The writer who embraces obstinacy travels down a similar path but never realizes success. The root cause of obstinacy is often bad advice. Bad advice sends us on crusades from which we may never recover.

THE KINGDOM OF MYTHIA

The wind blows differently in this part of the forest. I see rays of light through the bushes over there. Fellow writer, we have reached the end of this dreadful forest! Run as fast as you can and let's leave this place behind!

We've broken through the tree line into a clearing of wavering tall grass. The air is so much fresher here. Sun rays peek through the gray clouds. This sunset is most brilliant—orange, pink, yellow, and gray. It must be a good omen; I can feel it.

I don't know about you, but I am not going to miss that forest. The further we walk away from it, the more I relax. I prefer clean air, sunlight, and plenty of space to move. Hopefully, we never have to deal with shifting trees again.

Let's climb that hill over there. A large city lies below in the distance. Scenic and rustic, it might as well be painted onto the countryside. It's the kind of city that makes you want to write a fantasy novel. Gabled roofs, half-timber houses, helices of smoke rising here and there. This city is filled with horses, for I can hear their galloping and whinnying on the wind.

There is the royal palace—that great gray turreted castle

with black flags streaming atop the spires. I've never seen black flags on a castle before.

The city gates are open. Two guards dressed in black with swords stand like sentinels. They ignore us.

At least they allow us passage.

This city hustles and bustles. What a welcome sight after our time at the Tower of Laughing Beasts and Forest of Illusions. The people here walk with purpose. They carry knapsacks and look generally satisfied with their lives. A few stare at us because we must look like travel-worn foreigners, but I suspect foreigners are a regular sight here.

Fellow writer, someone calls you. A pudgy innkeeper with a mustache.

"Fellow travelers, you look weary. Care to stay at my inn for a day of rest and good food? My prices are reasonable."

The inn is a two-story half-timber building with a thatched roof, windows with diamond grids, and a sign with a hog's head on it. It looks as inviting as any inn we can find.

"Excellent, right this way. I have a room all picked out for you. How was your journey through the forest? Did you encounter any beasts? You won't encounter any beasts in the City of Mythia. His Majesty makes sure that the guards at the gates protect the city well. I haven't seen a beast myself in over five years. How's that for security? Here are my prices. What currency do you have? I see… Those are some strange coins, my friend. I've never seen them before. I ask that you travel to the castle. The king's staff has many currencies in supply. I'm sure they have seen those coins. Tell them you're staying with me and they will give you the right amount. Hopefully, there will be some left over for you. My lodging includes a comfortable room and meals for the day. I also have a bath you can use."

That innkeeper is a friendly fellow. I believe him about the security. Deposit your things in the room, take off your armor, and let's walk as commoners for change.

⊏⊐

The Royal Castle rises into the sky. It's far grander and taller than it looked from the hillside.

Curious that there are alligators in the moat. A pack of them sun on the banks underneath the castle. His Majesty must take his security seriously. There are even archers on the ramparts with arrows aimed at the entrance.

The portcullis rises as if to greet us. A wan-faced man in a black tunic is walking toward us. He must know why we are here. With his bowl haircut, sad eyes, and hands clasped together, I would have mistaken him for a friar.

"Good morning, travelers. What brings you to the castle today? Currency? Let me see your coins. Yes, we've seen those before. Where are you staying? Yes, the Hog's Head. A fine establishment if there ever was one. Albert makes the best chili in the city. It is not to be missed. Please give me your coins. Follow me into this courtyard. The guards probably didn't say much when you entered the city gates, did they? They've been instructed to be quiet and to speak only to beasts, which never happens. I welcome you to the Kingdom of Mythia. We are the greatest kingdom in the world. Our citizens live beast-free, and all are welcome. This courtyard is the Courtyard of Friendship. That fountain over there was designed by Her Majesty herself. It is a peace offering to all citizens. Anyone in the kingdom can come here to relax and enjoy this rose garden. We keep the lawns manicured and the air fragrant.

"Follow me through these arches. This castle was constructed by His Majesty's eight times great-grandfather. It has been passed down through the generations and we proudly maintain it. Why, it looks better than it did hundreds of years ago. The king demands it. We have arrived at the foreigner waiting room. Right this way. I will return presently with the proper currency for you."

Such a sumptuous room we stand in now, fellow writer. Those black tapestries with a yellow griffin woven into them hang high from the ceiling. You might as well have a seat on that wooden bench there and enjoy the fire crackling in the fireplace. Are those white grapes on the table next to the bench? Oooh, I wish I still had my physical body!

Even the napkins on the table are black. The silverware is stained black as well. Our king must love black. Here comes our castle tour guide.

"Here are your coins. This pouch contains 50 Mythic coins, the currency of our great kingdom. You will find that these coins last you a very long time here. But, may I ask you a question?"

I wonder what our friend has in store for us.

"We have seen your coins before, but it has been quite a long time since a warrior from your part of the world has come here. His Majesty himself would like to speak to you. Come right this way."

The king requests an audience. Now this is an interesting change in events.

———

The throne room is every bit as elegant as I expected. Long black carpet with golden fringes. Clerestory windows with rays of sunlight shining through and crisscrossing. Guards standing watch along the sides of the room. Terraced stone steps leading up to two thrones cast in gold.

The first throne is smaller and empty. On the second throne sits a small, quiet man, resting his head on a fist. His golden crown is bedecked with obsidian ovals. Seeing this man makes me want to cry, for his royal wear is all black, save for the golden ring on his finger.

He sees us now and perks up. Stand tall, fellow writer!

"Welcome, dear traveler. I hope that your first experience in the city has been a positive one. I am the king. It is my greatest honor to host you in the Kingdom of Mythia. I have hosted warriors from all over the world. They come here but never stay for long. As I remarked to my Exchequer, it has been quite a long time since we have seen one from your part of the world here. The last warrior from your land was an exceptional knight. Am I wrong to assume that you are exceptional?"

Here is a man who recognizes our talent in fighting beasts! Bow and say thank you.

"That is most excellent. I wish that you came to my kingdom under better circumstances, dear traveler. Unfortunately, I am in mourning. You see, this throne next to me is empty. It has been so long since my wife reigned next to me. I miss her wisdom. The beasts of this world abducted her and my daughter while they slept. I know not where my family is. I send scouts across this land once a fortnight to investigate and return to me with any news they find, but they have been unsuccessful. I swore to reunite my family, but I fear that I will fail. I need a good warrior to traverse this land and bring my family back to me. I am sorry to impose this upon you when you must be weary and hungry, but I am a desperate man. Can I ask you to help me? I will forever be in your gratitude."

I am flabbergasted, fellow writer. What a noble mission we have been asked to carry out. We are brave warriors. This is exactly the kind of thing we were meant to do. You must accept His Majesty's offer.

"I am already in debt to you. Thank you for your service. Keep those coins in your pocket. I will send word to the Hog's Head that you may stay there for as long as you need to carry out this mission. I will pay for you. In the meantime, get some rest, eat well, and begin your journey in the morning. I will send one of my staff to visit you and inform you of important details."

The king has tears in his eyes. He stands and bows to us. We must bow harder. His Majesty bids us farewell.

Perhaps this was the reason I was pulled from the afterlife to assist you, fellow writer. I knew another adventure would wait, but not one as urgent as this.

———

Our journey back to the Hog's Head Inn has been a satisfying one, fellow writer. I am glad we took the scenic route through the city to get to know it a little better. You must be tired by now after such a long day. To think that you started on the beach in a feat of survival and are now commissioned by the King of Mythia to save his family. Well done!

I smell the sweet, spicy aroma of chili coming from the Hog's Head. Our innkeeper must be hard at work in making his famous chili. If only I had my tastebuds!

The innkeeper is a true hunter. I have always appreciated taxidermy, but this man takes it to another level. I have never seen so many hog, deer, and goat heads in one room. That goat head over there is giving me a hairy eyeball. I don't think it has ever smiled in its life.

The other guests are gathered at the long tables in the eating hall. These men and women look like jolly companions. You shall have a good meal.

What a fragrant bowl of chili that is! It looks so good I could eat the spoon! I wonder what type of meat that is. Perhaps goat...

Look—a guest is bringing her bowl of chili and joining your table. She wears a purple tunic and has big brown eyes. Her hair falls to her shoulders. Do you see that amulet around her neck? Three concentric circles cast in silver. I wonder what strange land she hails from.

"I saw from the moment you entered that you aren't like the others around here. I come to you with a grave message."

Grave message? That's odd, fellow writer.

"Dear knight, how much of this city have you seen? That is what I feared. You have not been in this city long enough. Things happen here."

Yes, indeed. No land is safe, is it, fellow writer? Tell her about our mission from the king.

"You have made matters worse. This king—why hasn't he made any progress? Why did he choose you of all people? Please heed my warning. My message comes not from me, but through me. I will only be able to say it once."

Things are getting stranger, fellow writer. Maybe the chili has made her mad. Or, maybe she needs to eat some chili to change her state of mind...

Oh, dear—her eyes have rolled back into her head. She's extending her hands and floating into the air. Her body emits a faint golden glow!

"You will experience great hardship. Your life will never same. It is only a matter of time before you discover that my words were worth heeding. But you will not heed them. You will still embark on this mission, and you will realize your fate."

She speaks of fate. I really think that chili is affecting her, fellow writer.

"The mission you embark on is not what it seems—"

Stand back, fellow writer. Several guests have tackled the woman. She fights them and curses them. And her chili is all over the floor. What a tragedy.

The guests are carrying her out of the Hog's Head. They're telling her to get out and never come back for speaking so ill of the king.

"You are fulfilling fate! You all will rue the day that you

didn't listen to me. Fellow knight, please listen. Protect yourself—"

Two Royal knights have appeared. They are dragging her away kicking and screaming.

That entire encounter was strange, wasn't it?

⸺

I hope you had a good night's rest. I am sure you slept well with the Hog's Head chili in your belly. The room seemed quite comfortable to me. Though sparse, the bed was soft and comfortable. At least that's what you told me.

I hope you enjoyed your breakfast of eggs, bacon, and bread. I hope the king will send even better food with us on our journey.

What a fine morning. Rays of sunshine make the streets look as if they are paved with gold. A flock of crows just flew overhead. The smell of eggs is still in the air. I like this city very much.

Here come members of the king's Royal Guard. One is a knight riding a brown steed, and the other is the king's Exchequer. The Exchequer waves at us.

"Good morning, knight. I trust you slept well. Indeed, I thought as much when I heard you were staying at the Hog's Head and going to enjoy its chili. As His Majesty promised, we bring you provisions and information that you will find quite helpful in your journey. First, let's settle the provisions. You will take this horse. This is a fine Percheron stallion from the king's collection. Well-trained, valiant. Speed is its hallmark. You do know how to ride, don't you? Excellent. On the horse are two saddlebags with a fortnight of supplies. You'll find food, water, and money for the various towns and villages you will encounter. Next is a history lesson for you to understand. His Majesty was devastated upon the abduction of his wife and daughter. We miss the queen and princess terribly, and it would mean everything to His Majesty if you could recover them. But many warriors have come before you, and all have been unsuccessful. Your first destination should be south of the city. You will find a small village several hours from here that you can use to begin your investigation. Be thorough, and do not be deterred by anything or anyone. If any question your affinity, tell them the king sent you. I wish you well. May you go forth and peace and bring the royal family home alive."

DEATH MOUNTAIN

BEAST #26: FRAUD

Our journey begins, fellow writer! These plains are expansive and colorful as an old painting.

I like your steed. It strikes me as a faithful and dependable horse.

Here comes a smiling man. He wears hunter's wool and leather turnshoes.

"Hello, fellow travelers! It is great to see you again!"

I have never seen this man, fellow writer. Have you? I didn't think so.

"It's great to have you back. How did your journey go?"

Curious, don't you think?

"My friend, I told my village all about you and your bravery. I told them that a finer knight never existed. Have you any word of the royal family? No? Same as last time, then. Very well. I shall give you a pat on the back and a wish farewell. When we meet up at Albert's Inn, I will tell you stories of my travels! Take care."

Who was that, fellow writer? Such a strange conversation.

Say, didn't you have a pouch hanging on your waist?

That blasted scoundrel stole your money. Should we track him down?

Perhaps not. We will almost certainly end up in a fight.

You still want to track him down? Fine, let's pursue him. There he is, on that hill over there! You! Stop!

Good job, fellow writer. We scared him and he is on his back, crawling away. Let's see what this vagabond has to say about his crimes.

"Listen, don't attack me. I just did what I had to do. Here, take your money."

We have our money. That's all we need. Perhaps you should still draw your sword and scare him. Maybe he'll think twice about doing this to the next person.

"Please, don't kill me! I told you I was sorry! I gave you every bit of your money back. Don't stab me, please! I have children. They're the reason I do this."

There, you can sheathe your sword, fellow writer. If this man has a shred of honesty in him, then we will have taught him a lesson tonight. If he is a fool, well—there was nothing we would have been able to do anyway. He's running away now toward the City of Mythia. Good riddance to him!

Check your pouch—is all the money there?

It's not?

I knew it. How much is there?

Wait a minute—your pouch was maroon. This one is burgundy. They're similar but not the same. Those coins are also different. Look how they melt in your hand. They are but chocolate.

Quick, after him!

Wait—no, hang back, fellow writer! That man is not a man. He is a beast! His body has exploded into flames and he is now a phoenix, rising high into the sky with your money pouch in his mouth. There's no catching him now. He is criss-crossing the sun now. And he's gone.

We could send our dragons after him, but I suspect it is not worth the fight.

Fellow writer, it appears we have been defrauded. Our thief knew exactly what he was doing. He knew we would come after him and that we would have mercy on his soul.

He has made away with all of our money, and the only thing we have left is the king's provisions.

This is unfortunate, but we must persevere. I still cannot believe that man was a beast in disguise. That a beast can imitate a man is disturbing. I knew the beasts in this land were different, but now we understand why. Let's capture our learnings in a meditation.

A Meditation for Fraud

As long as there are people in the world, there will be fraudsters. Their timing will always be impeccable.

A fraudster usually attacks at two key moments in a writer's career:

- when they are at a high point
- when they are at a low point

Writers at high points are riding high and feeling invincible. They've just finished a novel or experienced an amazing career milestone, such as hitting a bestseller list or attracting international attention for their writing. At this point, the fraudsters smell the blood in the water and want to cash in on some of the author's success. They cloak themselves in opportunity and use that to strike. Your wallet will be lighter, you will have fewer copyrights, and you will be ashamed when you uncover the fraudster's true nature, which may not be for quite some time. By then, they will have been paid handsomely and the damage will have been done.

When you're at your lowest point, you are desperate for something, anything that will change your trajectory. Imagine losing your job and not having enough money to publish your books, or being diagnosed with a devastating illness that makes you question whether you can keep going. Or, a fight with a spouse that makes you determined to make your writing pay the bills even though you're nowhere near that yet.

That's when fraudsters strike. Usually, they use a scattershot approach and they just happen to find you receptive to their message. Their promises are exactly what you want to hear, and you are all too willing to give them your money, copyrights, and dreams. They will leave you ashamed, dejected, and with little faith in your future.

You must always be ready for fraudsters when they appear. Often, they disappear just as quickly as they arrive.

The best way to arm yourself against fraud is to accumulate knowledge. When you understand how things are, you are less likely to be defrauded. Fraudsters depend upon ignorance to further their trade.

An author who understands their craft and industry and who holds themselves out with self-confidence is anathema to a fraudster. They want easy, stupid prey.

Therefore, always seek knowledge and understanding of the best practices in your industry. Always be suspicious of people offering you opportunities, and do your due diligence and research before engaging. Not everyone in this world is a fraudster, but if you can avoid the bad guys, you will have a long, healthy career to show for it.

BEAST #27: STIGMA

We have been traveling south for several hours just like the king's man said. Down there in the valley, do you see it?

A small village. Not nearly as large as the City of Mythia, but quaint. Picturesque. The kind of place that a painter would illustrate. The only thing missing is the sea, and this would be a seaside village to die for.

Beyond the village is a tall mountain range with snow-crusted peaks. Something tells me we will be climbing one of those mountains. The one in the center is particularly menacing. Clouds wreath the summit.

But alas, we have come to the gates of this cute little village. Look at the homes with their thatch roofs! Pigs, dogs, and chickens run free in the street. Watch your step—not for the animals, but for what they leave behind.

Okay, so this village doesn't smell the greatest. It certainly has some sanitation challenges, but from afar, there is no greater picture of the countryside.

Children are running up to us, wanting to know who we are and where we're from. If only we had toys or confections to give them! These children are joyous. I don't think any of them has frowned one day in their lives.

See if you have something in the king's provisions that you can give them.

There are confections. I see no harm in handing them out. It might make us more endearing to the parents, who we will need for valuable information.

Let's engage that gentleman over there. Call him. Strange. He is walking away. Surely he heard you call him.

There is a woman over there tending to her chickens. Let's talk to her.

Why, she is walking away too! Very curious, fellow writer. Perhaps you should tell people that the king has sent you.

A man is eating some bread over there on that fence. Let's be clever and approach him from behind so that his only choice is to flee the village. He won't escape us.

Good job, fellow writer. We have scared the man, but he cannot run from us. Tell him the king has sent us.

"Sent by the king, are you? Yet another one."

This village must not be so loyal to our gentle king after all.

"You knights are all the same. You come here thinking that the world is your playground and that you are skilled in your abilities. This village used to produce the finest knights in the world. They were all under contract and specialized in the old ways. Those ways are truly better. You wandering knights have all the freedom you desire, but none of the respect. If you want our respect, then renounce your ways, join our village, and let us teach you the traditional ways of doing things. You don't ride your horse correctly. You don't hold yourself out correctly. If you were a knight 200 years ago, you wouldn't be a knight. So don't go thinking that just because you carry a sword and were *commissioned* by the king that you have any real clout in this world. Let me go, or you will regret it."

What a nasty man! This is a man who has no respect for

his kingdom. Screw the old ways of doing things. If they were so good, then why don't we continue doing them that way? That man was more than insulting—he was outright toxic. It seems we are not among allies.

Let's see if anyone else will engage us.

Everyone hurries away from us. It is a shame, for there is no difference between us and us and the knights they romanticize. What is true is that we are all human and we all have our preferences. Just because our preferences don't align doesn't mean we are evil.

Fellow writer, duck! A villager throws a stone!

More villagers are gathering with stones. Our entrance into this place is now well known. Keep ducking, fellow writer! Good thing you have your armor! We must return to the horse and flee. We will find no news of the king's family from here.

Push your horse as fast as you can. If only the king had told us about how disloyal these people were. We would have never stopped.

We are outside the village limits now. They can no longer harm us. They have stopped throwing their stones and they laugh as we gallop away.

I see our mistake. The village now glows in strange fire. Every person is engulfed in flames. The laughter and crackling carry into the air. It appears our village is infected by a beast.

No, fellow writer, don't turn back. To turn back is to fall prey to its trap.

See? Now we are defeating this piece by running away. The flames crackle and burn higher and higher and higher. The villagers' laughter has now turned to screams. The village is burning. Soon, there will be nothing left.

Fellow writer, let's turn away as the city burns to the ground...

It is now gone. What a damn shame. Were those people real, or was it an illusion of the beast? I wonder if our king knew about this. Heaven help the knights that tried to make progress in that village, for they will have never succeeded. Let's write our meditation.

A Meditation for Stigma

Some people will hate you simply for who you are and what you stand for. They will simply see the style and/or genre in which you write and instantly profess you to be a hack. They will seek cover under the old ways of doing things, but the old ways of doing things are not always the best way. In fact, sometimes our fellow writers cannot see that the old ways are damaging to them.

The result is that you may be stigmatized. People will see you as part of the problem or as someone to not be taken seriously. The secret is to let the stigmatized others live in their fantasy world. Become successful enough and no one will be able to deny you.

The worst thing you can do in the face of a stigma is to engage it. Trying to convert it is like trying to convert a vegan to eating beef. They will be so steadfast in their beliefs that they won't hear you. The best thing you can do is lead by example. In living and modeling the life you wish to live, you will inspire others to do so. Inspire enough people, and things will begin to change.

We will face stigma from critics, readers, and even other fellow writers. We must learn to live our best lives, and the opinions of others be damned. Only then will we minimize the presence of stigma in our lives.

BEAST #28: THE BEIGE ARMY

We have come to the foot of a mountain. I do not know how easy it will be to traverse it. That winding path up there may be more treacherous than it is worth, but we must obey the king's orders to be thorough in our search. According to the map, there is another village further up the mountain.

These foothills are steep. If I had my physical body, I would be grateful for the Percheron stallion on which you ride. The incline on the footpath grows steeper the further we climb.

I am glad that you have blankets and a coat in the king's provisions. God bless His Majesty for looking out for us. This is a man who knows his kingdom.

Up there. There is a man perched on that ledge. He is wearing a beige tunic. He is watching us. I wonder what he is up to. Let's hail him.

He is running away. Here we go again.

Perhaps that man is a beast. We just don't know anymore, do we?

Let's wind up this path and see where it takes us.

This mountain is expansive, indeed. We have come to a steep valley covered with grass and boulders. The bank on one side is quite high. An excellent place for one to keep watch.

As I expected—there is that man again. That beige clothing—I have never seen such garb before.

He runs again. We won't let him escape. We'll climb that rockface over there. We'll bid our trusty steed to wait here. He won't go anywhere.

I hate to make you climb, but I have a bad feeling about this man. We aren't going to let him spy and run.

Put one hand in front of the other on this rock face. Keep your foothold and make sure you don't lose your grip. I would hate to watch you fall to your death.

Very good, fellow writer. If I didn't know your knightly skills, I would have thought you were an expert rock climber. Color me impressed. If I had my physical body, I would be at the base of this cliff, staring upward in fright.

A few more feet and—success! We have come to the top of this cliff. Swing yourself over and take a moment to catch your breath.

A sea of tents stretch out before us. Warriors walk around in beige undergarments, laughing and talking. Their faces are common and unfamiliar.

They carry swords and arrows. The smell of roasted meat is in the air.

Someone sees us. He yells.

The soldiers are running to their tents now, suiting up and grabbing their weapons.

We have stumbled into a lion's den!

We should summon our dragons. Dragons! We need your help!

Watch out—they are shooting arrows.

Duck, fellow writer.

One of the men has uttered a war cry.

Here are our dragons. Climb aboard. We will take to the sky.

Dragons, barrel roll to avoid this army's arrows.

I'm tired of running away from this kingdom's residents. I don't care how many soldiers are in this army. We will stay and we will fight.

With two dragons and your skills, we will give them a lesson, for we are commissioned by His Royal Highness!

Dragons, fan over the battlefield so we can see who we are dealing with.

Those tents over there—they look like the tents of the commanders. Let's visit them, shall we?

Dragons, fly down there and burn everything in your sight.

A wave of fire sets the tents ablaze. The men in this Beige Army are screaming now. We surprised them. They expected us to run away.

A man has run out of the largest tent, waving at us. He is clad in beige. He has a beard, a mustache, and a scar on his face. Let's land and reprimand him.

Disembark your dragon, fellow writer. Keep your hand on your sword, but our commander is kneeling. It appears he is surrendering.

"Gentle knight, please accept my sincerest apologies for the attack. You are not the first knights we have encountered in this passage. When we first saw you, we assumed that you were like all the other knights that have passed through here. When you showed us your bravery and battle skills, we immediately realized our mistake. It is clear to me that you are an exceptional fighter. I now see the error of my ways, and I regret that we doubted you in the first place. Where are you going, knight?"

It is good that we have found allies despite our initial battle. Go ahead, tell him, fellow writer.

"His Majesty sends you, yes? It has been some time since we have been under his service. Our commander is the Critic.

We follow him faithfully. Perhaps he was wrong about you. Our scout saw you when you began ascending this mountain, and he sent word to the Critic. Our leader is probably penning a hit piece on you right now. That is unfortunate, but we will leave that between you and him. I will send another scout to our leader to advocate on your behalf, but I strongly suggest that you continue climbing the mountain to meet him yourself. My army will give you no more trouble. You have my word. Farewell, gentle knight."

Well done, fellow writer. We defeated the Beige Army without a single wound. We have our dragons to thank for that.

Dragons, you are released. Stay close as we ascend this mountain.

While we're here, you might as well ask the soldiers for a meal. It's the least they can do for the inconvenience; it will also make our provisions last longer. While we eat, let's write our meditation.

A Meditation for the Beige Army

When many people discover that you wish to be a writer, they will immediately try to dissuade you. They will say things like "There's no money in that," or "Everyone wants to be a writer," or "There are better hobbies," or worse, "There are better professions."

These words can come from anyone. Friends, family, colleagues, random strangers you meet on the street—this is why they are called the Beige Army, a term coined by Marianne Cantwell in her book *Be a Free Range Human*.

Members of the Beige Army don't like to stand out. They would rather have approval from society, and they want you to be beige with them. They see the arts and it scares them because of preconceived notions about how artists live. They give you admonitions not to scare you, but to get you to believe that art is not a viable path.

What you don't understand about the Beige Army is that they too are often people who chose not to realize their dreams because they were conscripted into an army in which it is their responsibility to grow ranks. They too have abandoned their dreams.

You must resist the attacks from the Beige Army at all costs. When you do, they will see your true talent. When you become successful, they will shift and act as if they had supported you all along. They will then become allies. But to get them to that point, you must continue living your best life, owning your craft, and walking the path to becoming a successful writer.

BEAST #29: FEAR OF DEATH

We were lucky with that Beige Army. We have now arrived at a mountain city. Small wooden homes are interspersed across the mountainside. Beyond, a beautiful valley in a patchwork of shadows, trees, and light. I have never seen such a scenic valley.

Let's lead our stallion into the village entrance and see what awaits us. If our luck is as bad as it was at the Village of Stigma, the village itself might be a beast. That would be unfortunate.

The footpath leading up to the village is well-worn but well-maintained. The homes here are sturdy wood.

Let's talk to that woman over there carrying a pail of water.

She's wearing brown and gray rags. The water in her pail is crystal clear.

"A knight. We don't see your kind that often around here. What brings you here? His Royal Highness sent you? The last of your kind who came here was also sent by His Majesty. I don't know what happened to him. These mountains are treacherous. You seem like a skilled fighter, but even all the skill in the world won't help you against the Critic. You haven't heard of the Critic, have you? Why, he commands the Beige Army. Have you met them? They did not kill you? Now that's an interesting development. The Critic won't like that. Wait a minute...I recognize you now..."

Here we go with people claiming to recognize us. This is getting predictable.

"The Critic already issued a proclamation against you. The proclamation said there would be a knight riding into the village on a Percheron stallion, accompanied by two dragons in the sky. He said that you would have conquered the Beige Army without spilling an ounce of blood and that you possess many skills. I can see now that he was right."

So, this woman does recognize us after all. That is most unsettling, fellow writer. It seems this "Critic" has us in his sights. At least this woman has a gentle disposition.

"I suggest that you keep moving, gentle knight. There will be some in the city like me who will not give you trouble; others will be deeply influenced by the Critic."

Ask her where we can find this critic. We must have a word with them.

"You wish to meet the Critic? That is bold. No one has ever met him, for he lives at the top of the mountain where conditions are inhospitable for all but a supreme being like himself. The mountain you're on is called Death Mountain, and it gets its name for a reason. Do yourself a favor and turn back now while the Critic is being kind to you. It is just a matter of time before he will unleash his magic upon you. We have never met a knight that has survived such an onslaught."

I was correct, fellow writer. We *must* find this Critic. He is the reason the Beige Army attacked us, and he is the reason this woman had a potentially sour opinion of us. We have no choice but to confront this man head-on. I suspect he is not loyal to His Majesty. The king will almost certainly want to know about the Critic's activities.

"I must bid you farewell, gentle knight. Good luck on your journey."

Such a kind woman, and good to see a friendly face after our last experience at the Village of Stigma!

Our provisions are sound and our energy is abundant. Let's continue our journey through this village and continue up the mountain.

━━

We are much further up the mountain now. We should camp here for the night. The air has grown colder, and the first snowflakes of our journey are in the air. We should build a fire and stay here for the night.

Fellow writer, are you okay? Your body shook for a moment and you cried out.

You have a strange look in your eyes. You're sure you're okay?

Okay, but I just wanted to make sure.

This mountain is strange, indeed. We should definitely stop for the night.

I can't stop thinking about the Critic. This is a man who means us harm.

The king provided an ax in his provisions. Let us chop down that small pine over there. Give it a good hit. That's the spirit!

I have encountered many naysayers in my career as a writer. Many meant me much harm.

Stand back, fellow writer, for the tree falls. Timber!

Wow, how the ground shook. There is no place in this world we can't survive. Dragons, come down and start our fire for us.

That was easy. Warm yourself up well, fellow writer. Our dragons will keep watch as we sleep. The snow falls more rapidly now. If it continues at this pace, there will be inches on the ground before sunrise. That will make our trip more treacherous, but alas, we cannot control the weather.

Sleep well, my friend.

You toss and turn in your sleep. No matter what position you lie in, you cannot get comfortable.

Eventually, you drift into a deep sleep.

The snow chills your bones. An aurora of purple, red, and green dances across the sky. The faint sound of bells jingles in the air. The dark blue starry sky is more vivid than you remembered, and when you sit up, Michael is no longer there.

The dragons are gone too. It is just you on this mountain, on the slanted land, under the falling snow, and in the crisp cold air.

You call out for Michael, but he isn't there. Slowly, the realization that he might have been called back to the afterlife creeps up on you, and you grow fearful. Your stallion is gone too. It has made off with all your provisions, and you have nothing to your name; just your sword, shield, and wits.

You stand and cup your hands over your eyebrows, staring down into the valley, hoping to see any sign of life—perhaps Michael or your stallion or the dragons, off for a quick jaunt to find something that will ultimately help you on your journey. But they are gone.

You call out, but it's just your voice in the valley. The snow deadens your sound even though you shout at the top of your lungs.

Your only choices are to descend the mountain back into safety or to climb.

Michael wouldn't have retreated. He would have charged

forward to scout ahead. So, you fasten your sword and shield and begin a long trudge up the mountain.

A few yards ahead, voices whisper to you. "Turn back now."

"Don't go any further."

"Death awaits you."

You look around for the source of the voices, but there is no one.

The slope up the mountain grows steeper with every step. It snows so furiously now that you look behind and see your footsteps disappear in the snow just as quickly as you made them.

Left blends into right, up into down, sky into snow, and suddenly, you lose your way.

You drop to your knees one last time, calling out Michael's name. Only the howling wind responds, and you realize that you are truly alone.

It's getting colder. Hypothermia is setting in. You never thought you could be this cold. Up here on this mountain, with no guidance, resourcefulness, or lucky break to save you, you accept that you will die.

Except you don't accept it.

Your heart races. You think about all the things you could have and should have done as a writer. You think about the beasts you failed to conquer. You fall back in the snow, stare up at the blinding sky one last time before closing your eyes and giving in.

⸻

You are back in the City of Mythia. Lakes of sunshine blind you, and you put a hand over your eyes until they adjust.

You are standing under the portcullis of the castle. A procession of city folk passes, all dressed in black. Several men are shouldering a heavy pine coffin. You smell its wooden aroma mixed with the decay of human remains.

A bugle plays a sad song. All around the castle, there is not a sound.

His Majesty stands high above on a balcony, weeping.

Why does he weep?

Someone stumbles and the box crashes to the ground. A body rolls out. You inch closer and squint until you realize it is you. Your body is cold and lifeless and pale.

You look down at your current body and realize that you are floating. You don't have feet anymore. Suddenly, all those things Michael said about being a spirit hit home. You throw back your head and scream into the endless blue sky.

Something nudges you awake. Your eyes open to a backdrop of a starry night lit with a dancing aurora. You are encrusted with snow. The frigid cold has soaked down into your bones.

You shoot up, panting. You look upon the concerned faces of Michael and the two dragons.

Fellow writer, you were having a frightful nightmare. I am glad you awakened, for I was getting worried. It is freezing outside, yet you burn with the warmth of a thousand suns. Tell me, did you see?

It is as I feared. When you fell asleep, your body convulsed terribly. I tried to wake you up. I had to resort to prayer. The moment I did, a colorless spirit streamed out of your body, laughing as it disappeared into the snow. You were possessed by a beast, I'm sure of it. That's why I asked you if you were okay earlier tonight because you had a strange look about you.

The beast hit you with an illusion that you had died. From what you describe, it must have seemed very real to you. I'm sorry that you went through that, but I am glad that I knew what to do. I will keep watch on you for the rest of the night. With this snow, we can't make any progress anyway. We'll wait for morning and calmer weather. In the meantime, let's write our meditation.

A Meditation for the Fear of Death

The fear of death strikes us all. It comes out of the blue one night, and we see our entire future laid before us as if it were a foretold prophecy.

The truth is that, for many of us, we will die with books unfulfilled, dreams unrealized, and immense sadness for everything we did not achieve.

The antidote to this fear is to keep living, and to do everything we can to ensure that we leave a legacy for our books and our families.

BEAST #30: THE CRITIC

The snow has stopped falling. Our journey up the mountain continues.

The air is rarer and crisper up here. It is a good thing you have excellent physical training, fellow writer. Climbing this high would be a death sentence for many. You are handling it well.

In the distance, the snow-powdered peaks of this mountain range loom like a watercolor painting. The wind shifts snowbanks and a brown hawk flies overhead, disappearing into a summit. The sound is dead up here, the only noise audible being your footsteps, which quickly disappear and do not echo.

The summit is in view. We must climb harder and faster.

If we find nothing up here, at least we will have the satisfaction of climbing the tallest mountain in this land. We will also, without a doubt, be able to give His Majesty a briefing that thoroughly covers every inch of this part of the kingdom.

Fellow writer—do you see that? A dastardly shadow at the top of the mountain. It reminds me of a Grim Reaper.

The shadow stands with its back to us, looking out over the mountain range.

Hand at your sword, fellow writer. I have a bad feeling about this.

We are only a few yards from the cloaked shadow now. It still won't turn around, but now it speaks in a deep male voice.

"You should have turned back. You sabotaged my army, journeyed through my land unwelcome, and you did not heed the warnings of the beast that resides on this mountain. You foolish writer! You do not know what you have done."

We have met our Critic. Now he turns around. He has a sallow complexion with hollowed-out eyes. He holds a quill and a scroll. The scroll contains your name, fellow writer. Below it, magical runes glow against the parchment. He is cursing you!

The Critic is holding up the scroll and chanting in Latin. Draw your sword!

Do you feel the ground shaking, fellow writer? Large green hands are pulling themselves out of the snow. Attached to those hands are giant green, wart-ridden bodies with potbellies that look as if they will make these beasts tip over. These trolls stand ten feet tall, and they are naked. Their clubs are ferocious and so is their lack of dental work! I certainly don't miss their fetid breath!

Wait—they look familiar, don't they?

Why, these are the very trolls that we fought in the Tower of Laughing Beasts! The Critic is a necromancer, and he has summoned them from the dead.

Look to nine o'clock, fellow writer!

Slash!

You gave that one a hearty blow.

Dragons, come to our aid!

The dragons are spraying the area with fire.

The Critic is still chanting.

Behind you! That troll has a club.

Good dodge.

Slash! *Slash*!

The ground shakes as these trolls fall dead in the snow for a second time.

We have a clean run at the Critic. Go, fellow writer.

POW!

The Critic has hit you with a magical blast and sent you sliding down the slope. Dig your sword in the snow, fellow writer, and get back up. Dragon, spray the Critic with fire!

Our Critic is distracted. This is your best chance!

Slash! Slash!

The Critic has dropped into the snow. He stares at a semi-circle of his own blood among the whiteness.

"I… have…failed."

The Critic's body is convulsing now. Stand back.

It blooms into the gnarled, four-legged body of a beast with a human head. The eyes weep tears of blood and it staggers in the snow before falling. The trolls shatter in bursts of light, and now all is silent.

The Critic has fallen. He was a beast, just like I thought. It amazes me how such a beast could have such a sway on all of the people in this region.

Let's say a prayer for our dear mountain.

Before that, do you hear a voice, fellow writer? It sounds like a little girl.

Over there, in the snow. Dragons, give us a small wave of fire.

Aha! The fire has burned away the snow to reveal a wooden trap door in the ground. A sturdy lock secures it. Strike it hard!

The lock has fallen away. Out comes a young girl wearing a tattered pink dress. A silver tiara rests upon her head. She cries tears of joy as she hugs you.

This is the Princess of Mythia!

"Gentle knight, I have waited for years for someone to rescue me. A few times, knights made it to the summit of this mountain, but every time, the Critic struck them dead. When I heard the Critic utter his last words, I knew my prayers were answered. You have my everlasting gratitude. But what I wish more than anything else is to see my father and mother again."

What a tear-inducing story, fellow writer! Dragon, protect our dear princess and deliver her to the king with a message of our compliments. Our king will be so overjoyed!

The princess waves as she climbs atop one of our dragons. The dragon lifts into the air, and is gone.

We did it. Now, we must find the queen. Before we descend this mountain, let's write our next meditation.

A Meditation for Criticism

There comes a time in every writer's life when criticism becomes personal.

There is one person in some corner of the globe who makes it their mission to dredge up the trolls of this world against the writer and their writing. Sometimes it will be because something you said insulted them personally; and/or it may just be that this person is full of vitriol and you are the most convenient person to lash out against.

In any case, you will be on the Critic's receiving end.

Every critic will influence a certain number of people in the world. You will never be able to control this. Instead, the best remedy is to ignore the Critic and their army of trolls. Ignore them by writing more words and living your best life. They will eventually look for an easier target.

Critics are just as skilled with words as you are, but they cannot often write creatively. They prefer to tear others down with their words instead of building them up.

Leave critics alone. Karma goes around.

THE VALLEY OF THE FORGOTTEN

BEAST #31: MISERLINESS

I must congratulate you again on another battle well fought. Hopefully, by now, the princess is reunited with her dear father, and our dragon is flying back to meet us.

Our journey down the mountain was quite relaxing now that the Critic is dead. We have left the snow far behind us and we have arrived at a beautiful valley filled with trees, waterfalls, and a calm river running through the middle. This mountain offers unparalleled beauty.

The character of this valley is markedly different; we are on the other end of the mountain range. Gone are the flat, expansive fields that greeted us on our first travels to Mythia. Beyond this charming valley lies marshes and shaded bogs. I know not what waits for us, but if our journey up Death Mountain has been any guide, we are likely to face even more deadly challenges.

Here comes another traveler. This man has wild hair that seems to have been pulled out in places. Tears stream down his cheeks. His lips contort into a desperate scream, and his tunic is a sad, tattered rag. He cries out for help.

"Someone help me! Oh, gentle knight, I am so glad to

encounter a friendly face on this terrible journey! I need your assistance. Something dreadful has happened, something for which only a trained knight can cure!"

He has grabbed your arm, fellow writer.

"Come with me. We must go quickly!"

This is odd, fellow writer. We should ask him what he wants. I have grown weary of travelers in this kingdom.

"There is no time to talk, for time is of the essence. You must hurry and I will explain on the way. Our journey will take two whole days, and I apologize if it takes you far off your path. But I will be forever in your gratitude. We shall take your horse. Let's go!"

Pull away, fellow writer. This fellow will need to solve his own problems.

"Why won't you help me?"

Tell him it's nothing personal, fellow writer, but this land is full of charlatans. We cannot afford to be led astray when the queen desperately needs our help. Go away, sir!

"Please! I beg of you. If you don't help me, I will—"

Be *gone*, good sir!

Come, fellow writer. Spur your stallion forward and let us leave this man behind. I have a bad feeling about him.

"Please, God, no!"

Look—the man is running away from us, across the valley. A giant beast with the wings of a hawk, a serpent's tail, and the shriek of a harpy is descending from the clouds. Now the beast has the man in its grasp and is carrying him over the valley. He's screaming.

The hawkish beast has carried him into the woods, where his scream is cut short.

Was this man a beast? We will never know, but I feel awfully bad about this. Had he told us what he wanted, we might have been more willing to help, but if he told us that he was being pursued by a beast, we wouldn't have listened to him anyway.

Fellow writer, I must apologize for my harshness. My only concern was to protect you, but I don't want you to take the wrong lesson from this. Allow me to give you a meditation.

A Meditation for Miserliness

This miserliness has nothing to do with money. It has to do with your spirit.

We accumulate knowledge and experience as we progress through our careers. In becoming more skilled writers, it is easy to forget our humble beginnings. We focus so much on solving the new problems of the day that we forget what it felt like to be a new and overwhelmed writer. As such, we harden our hearts and stop helping those who come to us. It is not possible to help everyone who needs our help, but that doesn't mean we shouldn't try to help others.

Never forget where you come from.

Never forget what it feels like to be that desperate writer.

Never forget what it feels like to receive sage advice from someone more experienced than you.

We are never too humble to seek or give advice. The universe places no limitations on either of these things.

Therefore, keep your heart soft, remain humble, and help those who you can.

BEAST #32: TEMPLE OF THE SACRED COWS

We have reached the bottom of the valley. We leave Death Mountain and its other brethren far behind. Thank goodness for our fortune!

The land now slopes and sags into hot, humid bogs.

Bogs are not my favorite, but hopefully, our travels through this one will not be long.

His Majesty has bred a horse with a remarkable temperament. It does not like these wetlands any more than we do, but onward it charges. We must follow its example.

This water is the kind of water that dysentery loves. I hope you have good genes, fellow writer.

Our second dragon has arrived overhead. Its victorious roar indicates that the princess was reunited with her father successfully. Thank you, dragon! We will see you soon on the other side of these marshes.

That is joyful news as we head into these dreadful blogs. At least there is something to be hopeful about on this leg of the journey.

The flies here are incessant, buzzing around even when you

give them forceful swats. The humidity makes your underclothes stick to your skin.

We may want to stop so that you can take off your armor.
No? You don't want to take it off? Very well. I don't think even
I could withstand the sweltering temperatures for so long. You
truly are a brave warrior.

The king provided a sharp machete in his provisions. Take
it and cut your way through the thicket, for it grows increas-
ingly dense here. Give those vines a good whack. There you go.

The king truly prepared us. That machete is razor-sharp.
The thicket is no match for it and your strong arm. This bog
will not hold us. Hop off your stallion and continue your
crusade. It will follow. The tree canopy grows thicker too.

Shadows fall and it is dark as day in here. We must charge
forward and keep our wits about us. I hope for our sakes that
we do not encounter any more travelers, for my heart cannot
take them.

Onward, fellow writer.

⊏══⊐

These bogs are insufferable. I am glad I do not have my
physical body, for it would be a difficult slog for both of us.

Through the branches there, I see something.

Do you see that faint outline of gold among all this green?
Something is over there. Keep hacking forward and we will see
what it is.

Why, it is a temple. One designed in the classical style, with
Greek columns, elaborate cornices, and marble walls. A golden
cupola with a statue of a goddess rises into the sky.

This temple is covered in vines and dirt. It looks neglected.
We may be the first travelers to gaze upon it in a very long
time, fellow writer. We should tread carefully.

The marsh has reclaimed the courtyard leading up to the

temple. There is a broken colonnade full of broken columns. I wonder what religion used to pray here. Back in its heyday, this temple must have been truly magnanimous. Now, it looks as if the bog will swallow it whole any day now.

Let's ascend the marble steps to the doors, which are sturdy wood with windows covered in iron grates. One of the doors is ajar. Push it, and draw your sword.

Watch that spider's web over there. A gang of very unfriendly spiders lives here. They skitter into the shadows.

From sun rays through the windows in the cupola, we now see what the ancients were praying to—statues of cows. I've never seen so many cows in my life.

There's a golden cow. A silver cow. A cow made of glass.

Each cow has something written on it in messy red letters.

Perfectionism.

Literary agents.

Critique workshops.

Sloppy first drafts.

That last one in particular has fierce curved horns!

I suppose we should leave. There is nothing more to see. You and I have surpassed the virtues that these cows represent.

Oh no. The ground is shaking again. That's never a good sign.

To your right—that golden cow over there has come alive, and it is stamping its feet.

The mosaic cow lows as it bows its head with gnarled horns.

Fellow writer, this temple is filled with beasts, and these beasts are the sacred cows! We must run!

There, out of the door, and back into the colonnade. Now I understand why those columns were broken.

Boom!

One bull has charged a column and broken it in half.

Fellow writer, look out!

Boom!

More columns are broken.

Your sword won't work on these cows. We will have to be smarter in how we approach this problem.

Hop on your stallion. The cows are forming into a stampede. We have disturbed their home.

Good to see you on the stallion. Let's retreat into the marsh, where they won't be able to follow as easily.

Our plan worked! The golden cow is stuck in the mud. It can't get out.

The others have followed and are now stuck too. These cows will wish they hadn't woken up from their slumber.

I'd say our work here is done, fellow writer.

One cow brays at us loudly. Do you see the madness and anger in his eyes? This beast is truly desperate. It is just as well.

The cow is sinking into the bottom of the marsh. The other cows will follow soon, and we won't have to listen to their lowing anymore.

The sacred cows are now where they belong—where no one can find them.

Good riddance to those beasts. Let's gather our thoughts and write our meditation.

A Meditation for Sacred Cows

Every profession has its sacred values. These values are accepted as true and woe to those who challenge them.

However, some truths are not truths. They are what Dean Wesley Smith calls "sacred cows." A sacred cow is a myth that may have been true at one time or never was, but writers cling to it because they desperately believe that going contrary to it will sink their careers.

Examples of sacred cows include:

- needing traditional publishers to be successful
- writing sloppy first drafts
- the belief that you need to outline to write well

Every writer has a different set of myths that they must learn to let go of. Failure to do so means to operate well beneath one's true potential.

But sacred cows live in a hallowed temple. They do not like to be disturbed. The moment an author who doesn't need them messes with the temple, they launch into a frenzy.

The best way to defeat sacred cows is to let them charge to their own death. Eventually, their temples will grow deserted and the foot traffic will stop as more authors learn that the cows are not worth worshipping.

THE MARSHES OF
STAGNATION

BEASTS #33 AND #34: COMPLACENCY

There is nothing more macabre and sadder than graveyards. We have arrived at one, fellow writer. The sign on the front gate says, "Graveyard of the Fallen." You should kneel and pay your respects to those who came before us.

Please observe a minute of silence for our former comrades.

―――

Very well. This place is littered with gravestones. A murder of crows circles a mausoleum over there.

The grass grows tall and unruly. This is not the type of place you want to be caught in after dark.

The solemnity of this place is awe-inspiring. That tells you the caliber of writers who have perished.

The gang of crows is gathering more thickly now over that mausoleum. Do you hear that screaming? Fellow writer, it sounds like a beast. Draw your sword and charge forward, for a battle awaits us.

Behind the mausoleum is another four-legged monstrosity

with blood-red eyes, and purple, leathery skin. Rivers of blood run down its body. Our beast is not long for this world. It sees you and scurries back through the grass. Do not give it a single inch. Stalk forward. We should end this beast's misery.

I will look away while you do the deed.

━━

That beast is history. One blow was all it took. I wonder if one of our gentle knights resting here wounded it.

It's hard to tell for sure, but this place is deserted.

Except for...

Another beast. Over there, behind that gravestone. Another leathery-skinned purple beast lying in the mud as if it were an alligator sunning on a hot day. It doesn't look happy to see us, but it can also do nothing about it. I will look away as you end it as well.

━━

Very well, fellow writer. Two victories without hardly lifting your sword! How does it feel to be so victorious?

I see you are enjoying this as much as I am. Our king will appreciate our service in this graveyard. In our report to His Majesty, we should tell him that this place needs good groundskeeping. It's the least we can do for the fallen.

Wait...I hear another scream. This one is human. A woman is screaming inside that mausoleum.

Quick, cut the lock!

Wham!

Be careful entering the vault. We have no idea what's in there.

Jump back!

A woman has run out. She wears a white dress and wears a golden crown encrusted with rubies, emeralds, and sapphires.

She throws her arms around you and kisses you on the cheek. Her Majesty, the Queen!

"Oh, gentle knight, you have saved me! I thought I was going to die. Those dreaded beasts threw me in the mausoleum and have kept me here. Every once in a while, I heard a knight approach, but the beasts always killed them. I was beginning to think I was going to die in that mausoleum until you came and saved me. Please take me back to my loving husband and we will reward you with all the riches you desire."

Congratulations, fellow writer. We have saved the queen. Such a beautiful woman!

Place her on the stallion so that she does not get herself too dirty. When we escape the bog, we will have a dragon deliver her home.

It feels good to leave that graveyard behind.

It is at times like these when we must stop and be grateful for what we have. But indeed, your skill and bravery are of the utmost quality. Those two beasts in the graveyard did not stand a chance against your sword. Why, no beast is a match for us after such easy battles! I say to all the beasts of Mythia, we are the best. We are always victorious, and no guile will ever change the fact that we will be successful in reuniting His Majesty's family once and for all. I hope all you beasts can hear my cry!

What do you think, Your Majesty? See, I've made you laugh. Then you agree!

I'm sure you agree too, fellow writer. What? You say that my words were not strong enough. Very well. I ask you to announce your greatness to this world of beasts in your own words.

Excellent. These beasts should run screaming from us. Further through the bogs, we go.

The thicket begins anew. We will need to sharpen the machete at the end of the night with the strop the king provided. His Majesty thinks of everything.

Fellow writer? Oh my God!

Why are you lying on the ground? Oh dear, that beast came out of the bog unannounced. It is a large alligator at least two men long. Its scaly armor is the color of vomit, and one of its orange eyes is gouged out.

It crept up on us while we were taunting the world. It has a mouth full of sharp teeth and jaws that could crack your armor. Get up, fellow writer. The beast slithers through the water for you.

No—it has changed course and is heading for our stallion.

We must protect Her Majesty at all costs. Throw that rock over there.

Wham!

We have distracted it from our stallion. Draw your sword and strike.

Watch your armor, fellow writer. On second thought, it is a good thing that you kept it on. Very wise indeed, for he would have surely destroyed you if you were only wearing your undergarments.

We must fight the good fight!

Stab it there between the eyes.

Good job! Our beast swims away in retreat. The queen is safe!

Wait—do you see that over there? It is one of the purple beasts that we encountered back at the graveyard. It is drinking at the water's edge.

Our alligator beast is swimming for it.

Crack! The alligator has struck, and it has the beast writhing in its jaws. Now we know where those wounds came from.

But now—the alligator has let the beast go. Why didn't it finish the job?

Fellow writer, I feel a pit opening up in the bottom of my stomach as that beast lopes away bleeding.

This alligator is one smart beast. It gives us a final glance as it sinks into the murky water and swims away.

Forward, stallion. We don't want to stick around in case that alligator changes its mind. Let's ensure Her Majesty's safety.

That poor, bleeding beast is going to stagger back to the graveyard where the next unsuspecting knight will find it. It will put the beast out of its misery, but that is the trap.

Let us write our meditation as we put distance between ourselves and that ghastly alligator. Please pardon us for a moment, Your Majesty.

A Meditation for Complacency and Lack of Due Diligence

We all like to win. It's even better when those wins are quick. Claiming victory makes us feel as if we are invincible. It makes us feel as if we have learned everything there is to learn about this life, and that no more action or effort is needed. Whatever beast needs to be slayed, we do it quickly, feel good about it, and let our guard down. Such are the hallmarks of complacency.

When one becomes complacent, it leaves them vulnerable to the attacks of other beasts. The lack of due diligence beast is particularly deadly.

When we become complacent, we stop asking the difficult

questions. We stop scrutinizing things like we once did. We become so comfortable that we are easy targets against ourselves.

This happens slowly, but then one day, that alligator will launch out of the murky water and claim its prize.

Therefore, you must remain diligent in everything you do. You are never experienced enough to stop learning. You must always keep your eyes open for trouble. And when trouble comes, you must spot it early.

Everyone is complacent at some point in their writing careers. This complacency is only fatal when we fail to realize that the journey of a writer never has a destination. It is always ongoing and we must always continue improving.

RETURN TO MYTHIA

BEAST #35: SELF-SACRIFICE

We have reached the end of these miserable bogs. I thank my lucky stars. Let us call the dragons.

Dragons, it is an honor to see you. As you can see, we have rescued another member of the royal family. Please escort Her Majesty the Queen back to the castle and report back when you have been successful. Protect this dear woman at all costs.

Let's bow to Her Majesty as the dragons carry her off.

Fellow writer, we have done the impossible. We have rescued the royal family from the deadly grips of the beasts of the Kingdom of Mythia. We must congratulate ourselves. But most importantly, we must return to His Majesty to share in what is most likely to be a tearful reunion of the happiest kind.

▭

The City of Mythia is such a welcome sight. As we descend the hills back to that great city with a castle, I am overwhelmed with joy. I hope you are too, fellow writer. This is far more successful than our adventure at the Tower of Laughing Beasts.

A procession of knights and residents awaits us at the city gates. They are cheering and throwing flowers into the air for celebration. The knights carry banners with your name on them.

You are a hero, fellow writer! It is about time that this kingdom recognized your amazing and everlasting talent.

The children surround you now, chanting your name.

The innkeeper at the Hog's Head stands in front of his tidy inn. He offers you a bowl of chili. Take it from him and enjoy that well-deserved sweet and spicy food of the gods. If only I had my physical body...

Knights on horses blow their bugles. Beautiful men and women dance down the street in celebration of your bravery. What a wonderful event under a mackerel sky and a kingdom filled with so much sunshine and personal warmth.

Let us take our accolades and wave at our admirers as we follow the long stone path to the castle.

The flags over the castle are still black. Perhaps His Majesty was waiting for us so that we could watch him lower them. That would be a great sight.

Through the portcullis we go, through the courtyard filled with flowers and topiary, through a colonnade of archways and stonewalls, and into the throne room, where our king dressed in black sits on his throne, with Her Majesty on his lap and Her Royal Highness the princess next to them.

The king waves. His wife stands. The three royals rise and bow to you.

"Gentle knight, I had a good feeling about you. You have reunited my family, and I will forever be in your gratitude. If there is anything you need—and I mean anything—you ask me. You will always eat for free and you will never want for anything as long as you are in the walls of my kingdom."

The princess steps forward and speaks too. She puts a hand on her heart. "And as long as I am future queen, you will enjoy those same benefits. My children will hear the tales of your bravery too. We consider you a lifelong family friend."

No bow is low enough, fellow writer. The truth is that, while we were all too happy to perform our duties as properly trained knights, this is what we would have done even if we were not brave warriors. Be sure to tell His Majesty that.

"Spoken like a true knight. Thank you."

Fellow writer, please ask the king why he still wears black and why the flags of mourning still flap over the castle. Isn't this supposed to be a joyous day?

"That is a very good question. You see, I am still in mourning. I was hoping that you could continue your service to me."

Continue our service? But we did what was required. What else could he possibly want? Who else could he possibly be mourning?

"I am afraid I have not been forthcoming with you. When I asked you to save my family, I did so with a heavy heart. I hated asking for help. I simply could not bear to also tell you about the other royals who were also abducted by beasts. My uncle and aunt—the Duke and Duchess of Mythia—were also abducted in their sleep. I would be forever in your debt and you would have my family's everlasting gratitude if you could save them. Also, my cousin—the Duke of Imagination—was also abducted while he slept. He has five children who also went missing. And lastly, I must inform you about our royal dog, Susan, who was carried away by a winged beast before my very eyes. I know that I have put you through a lot, gentle knight. Only you can save the royal family of Mythia. Can I ask you to continue your duties?"

This is strange, fellow writer. If we had to search every inch of this land already, why didn't he tell us about his missing family members at the beginning? Ask him when they were abducted.

"It is incumbent upon you to get moving by sundown if

you want to make the proper distance to the next valley. I will restock your provisions. This means so much to me!"

Next valley?

I do not wish to say no to a king.

I thought our journey was done. This king is a low-down, rotten, dirty—

What did you say, fellow writer? You told the king no? Good God, fellow writer. You also told the king to go stick his throne up his—oh my.

"What did you say to me?"

You probably shouldn't repeat what you said—oh. You just did.

The king is frowning now. It appears we have overstayed our welcome in his kingdom. He is growing to twice his size now. How is this possible?

"I opened my kingdom to you. I gave you everything you needed. I gave you everything you could have ever wanted, and this is how you repay me? With this insolence?"

The queen and princess are twice their size now too. Their mouths have morphed into dripping jaws of blood.

The royal family is a family of...beasts??!

The king is reaching for you. "I will ask you one more time, and you will say yes. In case you didn't understand what I said, I wasn't asking you a question. Will you continue your duties to me to save the rest of the royal family? Answer correctly."

Fellow writer, you have decided to introduce some profanity into the conversation. I must agree. You also tell His Majesty to stick that throne up his—

"No! This wasn't supposed to happen! You are a foolish, foolish knight! I curse you and everything you and your ghost mentor stand for!"

So, he knew about me all along. This whole thing was a ruse.

The king is melting. So are the queen and princess. They're

melting into piles of coagulated blood that flakes off like snow and drifts across the throne room.

The walls are shaking. The castle is crumbling. Let's get out of here!

▭

Let's ride the stallion out of the city. Dear stallion, we need you now more than ever!

Run, run as fast as you can. Drive the horse forward, fellow writer!

The city melts around us. The residents we knew and loved were but clay simulacrums of men and women. Even the children kneel before our eyes into piles of dust and wax.

Go, fellow writer! The city will soon be no more.

My God! The stallion is melting beneath you too now. Jump off and finish the run on foot.

We have cleared the city gates. Fellow writer, the City of Mythia is no more. It has collapsed into the prairie as if it never existed. We are now all alone in this strange land.

Look—for the grass withers and dies too. The forest that we came through is melting into a flat landscape of dirt. I cannot believe my eyes. This land was a complete illusion.

A wall of hot air moves in and slams into us. We stand in the middle of a desert. Rolling dunes, shifting sands, and heat are worse than anything we have experienced thus far.

The Kingdom of Mythia was just that—a myth.

▭

Hours and hours have passed walking through this desert, but we haven't encountered a single beast. We must at least be grateful for that.

The desert is ending. We have come to the shores of

another sea. These waves are calmer. The waters are bluer and the surf gentler.

Do you see that shining city across the water?

It is a white, resplendent city on a cliffside. It radiates with the fullness of energy and positivity. My soul vibrates to its frequency.

It is your home. This place, unlike Mythia, is real.

You will have to swim across the water, but if you cast off your armor, I know you can do it!

My body is humming with spiritual energy. I am so happy for you, my friend, but it appears my return among the living is finished.

The afterlife is calling me home. Besides, I must have coffee with Ray Bradbury. Robert Louis Stevenson awaits me too!

Fellow writer, it has been the greatest honor of my afterlife to fight alongside you on another adventure. My compliments to you for another series of battles well fought. I trust that you will be able to handle this last battle by yourself. If you can defeat a new battery of beasts, then you can make it that small distance across the sea to the next chapter of your writing life.

Farewell, my friend, and may we meet again when it is your time to ascend to the next plane of existence.

As I fade, let's write our final meditations. I remind you of that great beast Self-Doubt, for you will surely encounter it again.

A Meditation for Self-Sacrifice

When we become successful, others will ask things of us. They will ask for help, support, time, and money.

It is a blessing to be in such a position. It can also be a curse.

Beware of giving away too much of your time. While you should avoid the lurch to miserliness, you should also avoid the opposite problem: self-sacrifice. You can sacrifice so much that your writing suffers.

Therefore, find the right balance, and know when to say no.

You may find that helping others sends you on a long, winding journey in which you realize that you have sacrificed too much in the end. Take from these journeys the lessons that you can and know when to end them.

A Meditation for Self-Doubt (Redux)

The great invisible enemy. No beast you face will be more powerful than Self-Doubt. It is a force multiplier whose presence makes all other negative emotions stronger and more resilient.

If you doubt yourself, you doubt everything.

The only way through self-doubt is to have faith. You must fight and question every negative thought.

This world is full of self-doubters. In doubting themselves, they harm others as well as themselves.

Your goal should be to avoid harm—harm to yourself and harm to others. Self-doubt dies in the intense heat of self-love. It may seem strange to love yourself, but chances are you haven't learned how to do that. Self-doubt fills the space where love has yet to burn.

You may think you can conquer self-doubt, but it is the great regenerator—it will strike at your moments of highest confidence. It will cast you from your tower of personal power, forcing you to climb it all over again.

You must ask: who am I? Why do I write? How can I love

myself better? How can I push this beast out of my life once and for all? Every day will be a battle, but you'll conquer self-doubt one day.

BEAST #36: SELF-DOUBT (REDUX)

You cast off your armor and throw it on the sand. A warm wind blows, ruffling your linen underclothes. You will need new clothes when you make it to the shining city, but that's the least of your concerns now.

You strap your sword and shield onto your back, take a deep breath, and dive into the cool water. It instantly refreshes and nourishes you. You take one last look behind you at the land of Mythia. You will be glad if you never see it again.

A few strokes later and you have found your rhythm. You glide through the water. This will be an easy swim. All you have to do is keep going.

You hold the shining white city as your guiding star, cupping your hands into blades and kicking your feet behind you like propellers. Nothing will stop you from claiming your prize.

Then, something grabs your ankle from below and wraps around it tightly, cutting off your circulation. It pulls you under.

Far, far below, you see a grinning squid with triangular teeth. A purple tentacle has clapped around your ankle.

Fear.

You grab your sword and drive it into the tentacle. The beast retreats into the depths of the sea.

You pick up your pace and swim faster than you thought you could. This is going to be a long journey across the sea— longer than you thought.

You hear another laugh behind you. The waves around you shake and turn into choppy breaks. Gray clouds appear out of nowhere and a fierce thunderstorm rumbles over the sea.

The waves toss you back and forth as a sinister laugh fills the air. The cold water splashes on your face.

Behind you, the desert shifts and rises upward.

You watch in horror as the island morphs into the beast that almost killed you last time. It grows bigger and bigger and casts a long shadow over the ocean.

It calls your name, and you raise your sword to it, giving a war cry.

Self-doubt has returned to settle the score, and you swim toward it to begin the fight of your life.

THE END.

READ NEXT: THE INDIE AUTHOR ATLAS

YOUR PASSPORT TO THE FIVE CONTINENTS OF THE WRITING WORLD

. . .

Have you ever felt overwhelmed by the sheer amount of information you have to learn as a writer?

The Indie Author Atlas eliminates overwhelm and makes the art of learning to be a writer fun. It turns the major concepts writers need to learn into can't-miss vacation destinations.

Ready to get away?

- Pamper yourself at the pristine beachfronts at the **Strategy Islands**
- Get lost in the expansive continent of **Craft**
- Discover new marketing strategies in the desert continent of **Marketstan**
- Tap into your inner entrepreneur in the sacred **Lands of Distribution**
- And more!

This quirky and engaging guide is written in the style of a travel guide, and it also has illustrated maps for each continent.

The Indie Author Atlas is unlike any other book for writers you've ever read. Relax and have fun as you wander through the amazing continents of the writing life. You just might learn something.

Get your copy today at www.authorlevelup.com/atlas.

MEET M.L. RONN

Science fiction and fantasy on the wild side!

M.L. Ronn (Michael La Ronn) is the author of many science fiction and fantasy novels including *The Good Necromancer*, *Android X*, and *The Last Dragon Lord* series.

In 2012, a life-threatening illness made him realize that storytelling was his #1 passion. He's devoted his life to writing ever since, making up whatever story makes him fall out of his chair laughing the hardest. Every day.

Learn more about Michael
www.authorlevelup.com (for writers)
www.michaellaronn.com (fiction)

MORE BOOKS BY M.L. RONN

Books for Writers

Indie Author Confidential (Series)
    How to Write Your First Novel
    Be a Writing Machine
    Mental Models for Writers
    The Indie Writer's Encyclopedia
    The Indie Author Atlas
    The Indie Author Bestiary
    The Reader's Bill of Rights
    The Self-Publishing Compendium
    150 Self-Publishing Questions Answered
    Authors, Steal This Book
    The Indie Author Strategy Guide
    How to Dictate a Book
    Advanced Author Editing
    Keep Your Books Selling
    The Author Estate Handbook
    The Author Heir Handbook

Interactive Fiction: How to Engage Readers and Push the Boundaries of Story Telling
Indie Poet Rock Star
Indie Poet Formatting
2016 Indie Author State of the Union

More Books for Writers:

www.authorlevelup.com/books

Fiction:

www.michaellaronn.com/books

APPENDIX: MEDITATIONS FOR EACH BEAST

A Meditation for Fear (Redux)

Fear is an ever-morphing and omnipresent foe. You can never get rid of it; you can only stave it off for a time. It will always return no matter what you do, and it will always show up unannounced at the worst time.

Though it is an ever-morphing foe, its weaknesses are the same:

- **Action**. Fear strives to stop you from taking action. The moment you take action, it has no hold over you.
- **Words**. As long as you keep writing, fear will retreat. Fear despises progress in your work, and with every word you write, it swears to return with revenge twofold.
- **Resourcefulness**. Fear doesn't like when you think out of the box. Sometimes, this breeds more fear, but by daring to be courageous, you will weaken it.

With the help of our friends and comrades, fear cannot realize its dreams; in its retreat, we realize ours.

A Meditation for Uncertainty

Beware the siren song of uncertainty. It is a beast that controls you from beyond.

No matter how many beasts you have conquered, you will one day end up on the shores of isolation. You will battle with fear and succeed. Then, one day, you will need to make a decision and you won't know where to start. The information you need will be unavailable, and you will feel as if you are on a razor blade, with success on one end and failure on the other. The only difference between the two is luck.

Uncertainty will sing to you and intoxicate you. You won't know what to do other than to sway like a cobra to the rhythm of Uncertainty's song. Sway too long and you will find yourself at the bottom of the sea.

We are all taken by Uncertainty's song from time to time. The key is to recognize when we are swaying. The sooner we recognize it, the sooner we can break her spell.

Sometimes, the best thing to do in light of limited information is to trust our gut, act with conviction, and be kind to ourselves if our decision doesn't get us the result we planned for.

Perhaps writing that book wasn't as successful as you thought it would be. Or, the marketing campaign you thought would catapult your book up the charts fails miserably. Or, you choose a cover that doesn't sell.

The reality is that in an alternate universe, you could be wildly successful if you had made just one decision differently. That's painful to think about. Visualizing ourselves in these different dimensions is what causes uncertainty. No one wants to end up in the dimension where they fail, but failure is an excellent teacher.

Be decisive in all things you do, own your decisions, and learn from them.

A Meditation for Bad Advice

Everyone has advice. Everyone loves to give advice freely. Sometimes, the advice is well taken; other times, it is not.

There are three types of advice:

1. **Advice that's meant for you**. This advice is right on time and perfect for your situation when you hear it.
2. **Advice that is not meant for you**. This advice is a bad fit for your situation *at any time*.
3. **Advice that you're not ready for yet**. This advice may seem like a bad fit, but it will be a good fit in time.

True wisdom is knowing what type of advice you are receiving at any time.

Most advice is bad advice. Advice that we're not ready for yet is more frequent than we think. But good advice—the advice that helps you take your skills to the next level—is the rarest of all. You must search for it like a lost diamond ring in a big forest. You walk and walk and walk, and just when you think you aren't going to find it, a glimmer on the forest floor catches your eye.

Develop a filter for advice. Ask yourself if advice is appropriate for you and your situation at the time. Also, ask how the advice feels. If something doesn't feel good, it's probably not a fit. Some mentors challenge us to do things we didn't think we could do, but there's a difference between that and advice that tries to shoehorn you into a particular activity, such as a marketing style that doesn't jibe with your aesthetic.

Good advice is advice that makes you think "Wow, I never considered that," or "Wow, why didn't I think of that to begin with?" Good advice helps you realize your true potential.

Because everyone has advice and loves to give it freely, we are oversaturated with it. Some advice-givers are indeed bad actors, but most often, they're just trying to help people in their own way, and they don't understand the impact that their advice would have on you personally. Therefore, it is your responsibility to develop a filter.

Filter out bad advice and you will gain clarity and calm.

A Meditation for Obstinacy

When we make up our minds to do something, sometimes we set out to do it no matter the consequences. We don't realize that we are charging down the wrong path. Others see our escapade for what it is and try to warn us, but we don't listen. Only during a low moment do we gain clarity about what we've done. At that point, there are two possible reactions: shame or anger.

Those who feel shame wear it like a battle scar. Sometimes, the shame is so great that writers quit.

Anger causes us to lash out at those trying to warn us.

Where things get complicated is whether you are traveling down the right path and whether the people warning you are giving good advice.

There is a thin line between obstinacy and dogged determination.

A writer who is doggedly determined eventually succeeds. Their failure to listen to others and insistence on doing things their way is what ultimately makes them successful. The writer who embraces obstinacy travels down a similar path but never realizes success. The root cause of obstinacy is often bad advice. Bad advice sends us on crusades from which we may never recover.

A Meditation for Fraud

As long as there are people in the world, there will be fraudsters. Their timing will always be impeccable.

A fraudster usually attacks at two key moments in a writer's career:

- when they are at a high point
- when they are at a low point

Writers at high points are riding high and feeling invincible. They've just finished a novel or experienced an amazing career milestone, such as hitting a bestseller list or attracting international attention for their writing. At this point, the fraudsters smell the blood in the water and want to cash in on some of the author's success. They cloak themselves in opportunity and use that to strike. Your wallet will be lighter, you will have fewer copyrights, and you will be ashamed when you uncover the fraudster's true nature, which may not be for quite some time. By then, they will have been paid handsomely and the damage will have been done.

When you're at your lowest point, you are desperate for something, anything that will change your trajectory. Imagine losing your job and not having enough money to publish your books, or being diagnosed with a devastating illness that makes you question whether you can keep going. Or, a fight with a spouse that makes you determined to make your writing pay the bills even though you're nowhere near that yet.

That's when fraudsters strike. Usually, they use a scattershot approach and they just happen to find you receptive to their message. Their promises are exactly what you want to hear, and you are all too willing to give them your money, copyrights, and dreams. They will leave you ashamed, dejected, and with little faith in your future.

You must always be ready for fraudsters when they appear. Often, they disappear just as quickly as they arrive.

The best way to arm yourself against fraud is to accumulate knowledge. When you understand how things are, you are less likely to be defrauded. Fraudsters depend upon ignorance to further their trade.

An author who understands their craft and industry and who holds themselves out with self-confidence is anathema to a fraudster. They want easy, stupid prey.

Therefore, always seek knowledge and understanding of the best practices in your industry. Always be suspicious of people offering you opportunities, and do your due diligence and research before engaging. Not everyone in this world is a fraudster, but if you can avoid the bad guys, you will have a long, healthy career to show for it.

A Meditation for Stigma

Some people will hate you simply for who you are and what you stand for. They will simply see the style and/or genre in which you write and instantly profess you to be a hack. They will seek cover under the old ways of doing things, but the old ways of doing things are not always the best way. In fact, sometimes our fellow writers cannot see that the old ways are damaging to them.

The result is that you may be stigmatized. People will see you as part of the problem or as someone to not be taken seriously. The secret is to let the stigmatized others live in their fantasy world. Become successful enough and no one will be able to deny you.

The worst thing you can do in the face of a stigma is to engage it. Trying to convert it is like trying to convert a vegan to eating beef. They will be so steadfast in their beliefs that they won't hear you. The best thing you can do is lead by example. In living and modeling the life you wish to live, you will inspire others to do so. Inspire enough people, and things will begin to change.

We will face stigma from critics, readers, and even other fellow writers. We must learn to live our best lives, and the opinions of others be damned. Only then will we minimize the presence of stigma in our lives.

A Meditation for the Beige Army

When many people discover that you wish to be a writer, they will immediately try to dissuade you. They will say things like "There's no money in that," or "Everyone wants to be a writer," or "There are better hobbies," or worse, "There are better professions."

These words can come from anyone. Friends, family, colleagues, random strangers you meet on the street—this is why they are called the Beige Army, a term coined by Marianne Cantwell in her book *Be a Free Range Human*.

Members of the Beige Army don't like to stand out. They would rather have approval from society, and they want you to be beige with them. They see the arts and it scares them because of preconceived notions about how artists live. They give you admonitions not to scare you, but to get you to believe that art is not a viable path.

What you don't understand about the Beige Army is that they too are often people who chose not to realize their dreams because they were conscripted into an army in which it is their responsibility to grow ranks. They too have abandoned their dreams.

You must resist the attacks from the Beige Army at all costs. When you do, they will see your true talent. When you become successful, they will shift and act as if they had supported you all along. They will then become allies. But to get them to that point, you must continue living your best life, owning your craft, and walking the path to becoming a successful writer.

A Meditation for the Fear of Death

The fear of death strikes us all. It comes out of the blue one night, and we see our entire future laid before us as if it were a foretold prophecy.

The truth is that, for many of us, we will die with books unfulfilled, dreams unrealized, and immense sadness for everything we did not achieve.

The antidote to this fear is to keep living, and to do everything we can to ensure that we leave a legacy for our books and our families.

A Meditation for Criticism

There comes a time in every writer's life when criticism becomes personal.

There is one person in some corner of the globe who makes it their mission to dredge up the trolls of this world against the writer and their writing. Sometimes it will be because something you said insulted them personally; and/or it may just be that this person is full of vitriol and you are the most convenient person to lash out against.

In any case, you will be on the Critic's receiving end.

Every critic will influence a certain number of people in the world. You will never be able to control this. Instead, the best remedy is to ignore the Critic and their army of trolls.

Ignore them by writing more words and living your best life. They will eventually look for an easier target.

Critics are just as skilled with words as you are, but they cannot often write creatively. They prefer to tear others down with their words instead of building them up.

Leave critics alone. Karma goes around.

A Meditation for Miserliness

This miserliness has nothing to do with money. It has to do with your spirit.

We accumulate knowledge and experience as we progress through our careers. In becoming more skilled writers, it is easy to forget our humble beginnings. We focus so much on solving the new problems of the day that we forget what it felt like to be a new and overwhelmed writer. As such, we harden our hearts and stop helping those who come to us. It is not possible to help everyone who needs our help, but that doesn't mean we shouldn't try to help others.

Never forget where you come from.

Never forget what it feels like to be that desperate writer.

Never forget what it feels like to receive sage advice from someone more experienced than you.

We are never too humble to seek or give advice. The universe places no limitations on either of these things.

Therefore, keep your heart soft, remain humble, and help those who you can.

A Meditation for Sacred Cows

Every profession has its sacred values. These values are accepted as true and woe to those who challenge them.

However, some truths are not truths. They are what Dean Wesley Smith calls "sacred cows." A sacred cow is a myth that may have been true at one time or never was, but writers cling to it because they desperately believe that going contrary to it will sink their careers.

Examples of sacred cows include:

- needing traditional publishers to be successful
- writing sloppy first drafts
- the belief that you need to outline to write well

Every writer has a different set of myths that they must learn to let go of. Failure to do so means to operate well beneath one's true potential.

But sacred cows live in a hallowed temple. They do not like to be disturbed. The moment an author who doesn't need them messes with the temple, they launch into a frenzy.

The best way to defeat sacred cows is to let them charge to their own death. Eventually, their temples will grow deserted and the foot traffic will stop as more authors learn that the cows are not worth worshipping.

A Meditation for Complacency and Lack of Due Diligence

We all like to win. It's even better when those wins are quick. Claiming victory makes us feel as if we are invincible. It makes us feel as if we have learned everything there is to learn about this life, and that no more action or effort is needed. Whatever beast needs to be slayed, we do it quickly, feel good about it, and let our guard down. Such are the hallmarks of complacency.

When one becomes complacent, it leaves them vulnerable to the attacks of other beasts. The lack of due diligence beast is particularly deadly.

When we become complacent, we stop asking the difficult

questions. We stop scrutinizing things like we once did. We become so comfortable that we are easy targets against ourselves.

This happens slowly, but then one day, that alligator will launch out of the murky water and claim its prize.

Therefore, you must remain diligent in everything you do. You are never experienced enough to stop learning. You must always keep your eyes open for trouble. And when trouble comes, you must spot it early.

Everyone is complacent at some point in their writing careers. This complacency is only fatal when we fail to realize that the journey of a writer never has a destination. It is always ongoing and we must always continue improving.

A Meditation for Self-Sacrifice

When we become successful, others will ask things of us. They will ask for help, support, time, and money.

It is a blessing to be in such a position. It can also be a curse.

Beware of giving away too much of your time. While you should avoid the lurch to miserliness, you should also avoid the opposite problem: self-sacrifice. You can sacrifice so much that your writing suffers.

Therefore, find the right balance, and know when to say no.

You may find that helping others sends you on a long, winding journey in which you realize that you have sacrificed too much in the end. Take from these journeys the lessons that you can and know when to end them.

A Meditation for Self-Doubt (Redux)

The great invisible enemy. No beast you face will be more powerful than Self-Doubt. It is a force multiplier whose presence makes all other negative emotions stronger and more resilient.

If you doubt yourself, you doubt everything.

The only way through self-doubt is to have faith. You must fight and question every negative thought.

This world is full of self-doubters. In doubting themselves, they harm others as well as themselves.

Your goal should be to avoid harm—harm to yourself and harm to others. Self-doubt dies in the intense heat of self-love. It may seem strange to love yourself, but chances are you haven't learned how to do that. Self-doubt fills the space where love has yet to burn.

You may think you can conquer self-doubt, but it is the great regenerator—it will strike at your moments of highest confidence. It will cast you from your tower of personal power, forcing you to climb it all over again.

You must ask: who am I? Why do I write? How can I love myself better? How can I push this beast out of my life once and for all? Every day will be a battle, but you'll conquer self-doubt one day.